God Makes the World

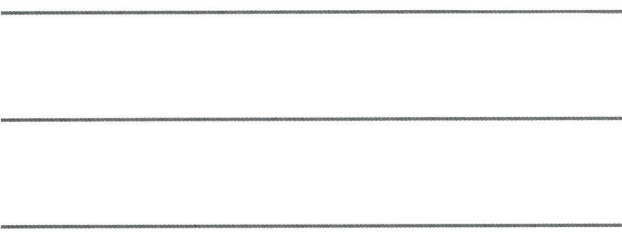

This
Bible Story Time book
belongs to

_____

_____

_____

Text by Sophie Piper
Illustrations copyright © 2005 Estelle Corke
This edition copyright © 2014 Lion Hudson

The right of Estelle Corke to be identified as the illustrator of this work has been asserted by her in accordance with the Copyright, Designs and Patents Act 1988.

All rights reserved. No part of this publication may be reproduced or transmitted in any form or by any means, electronic or mechanical, including photocopy, recording, or any information storage and retrieval system, without permission in writing from the publisher.

Published by Lion Children's Books
an imprint of
Lion Hudson plc
Wilkinson House, Jordan Hill Road,
Oxford OX2 8DR, England
www.lionhudson.com/lionchildrens

ISBN 978 0 7459 6946 6

First edition 2005
This edition 2014

This book is part of a box set and is not to be sold separately

A catalogue record for this book is available from the British Library

Bible Story Time

God Makes the World

Sophie Piper ✽ Estelle Corke

LION
CHILDREN'S

Imagine a dark and stormy night.

Imagine a dark and stormy sea.

Before the world began, there was only darkness and storm.

Then God spoke: "Let there be light."

The light shone. God had made the very first day.

On the second day, God spoke again: "Let there be sky above and sea below." And there was.

"Next," said God, "I want land as well as sea."

At once the land appeared. Plants began to grow: some were tiny; some were tall.

"I have worked for three days, and everything is very good," said God.

On day four, God made the sun. "You must shine through the day," said God.

"Moon and the stars: I want you to shine at night."

The whole universe did what God commanded.

Early on the fifth morning, God made all kinds of sea creatures: they came darting and diving through the waves.

Then God made the birds. They flapped and flew in the clear air.

On the sixth day, God made the animals – all kinds of amazing animals.

"And last," said God, "I shall make human beings. They will take care of my world."

The six days of making were over.
It was time for a day of rest.

The first man was named Adam. The first woman was named Eve. God gave them a garden home.

"Everything is for you," said God. "There is just one tree you must not touch. If you eat its fruit, everything will go wrong."

Adam and Eve were happy in their paradise home.

One day, a snake came and spoke to Eve. "Did God say you mustn't eat the fruit here?" it asked.

"Only the fruit from one tree," replied Eve. "If we eat that, everything will go wrong."

The snake twisted and wriggled. "Not true!" it said. "The fruit will make you as wise as God. Go on. Try it!"

Eve reached up. She picked the forbidden fruit. She ate some.

"It's good," she said. "I shall give some to Adam."

Adam took a bite. Then he and Eve looked at each other.

"Oh dear," they cried.

"We're both naked," said Eve.

"And now, for the first time, that doesn't seem right," said Adam.

They spent the day making clothes from leaves. Then they heard God coming. They hid among the trees.

God called them.

God found them.

God saw what had happened, and God was sad.

"Now everything must change," said God. "You must say goodbye to paradise. You must go out into the wide world. There you will work for all the things you need."

God made Adam and Eve clothes to wear.

Sadly they walked out of the garden.

As they looked back, they saw an angel with a sword. The blade flashed this way and that. They could not go to the garden ever again.

They looked ahead. "There are lots of weeds here," said Adam. "But if we work hard, we can plant crops. We'll manage."

Eve wiped away a tear. "It's sad not being friends with God," she said. "I hope this mistake is put right one day."

Noah and the Flood

This
Bible Story Time book
belongs to

_____

_____

_____

Text by Sophie Piper
Illustrations copyright © 2005 Estelle Corke
This edition copyright © 2014 Lion Hudson

The right of Estelle Corke to be identified as the illustrator of this work has been asserted by her in accordance with the Copyright, Designs and Patents Act 1988.

All rights reserved. No part of this publication may be reproduced or transmitted in any form or by any means, electronic or mechanical, including photocopy, recording, or any information storage and retrieval system, without permission in writing from the publisher.

Published by Lion Children's Books
an imprint of
Lion Hudson plc
Wilkinson House, Jordan Hill Road,
Oxford OX2 8DR, England
www.lionhudson.com/lionchildrens

ISBN 978 0 7459 6946 6

First edition 2005
This edition 2014

This book is part of a box set and is not to be sold separately

A catalogue record for this book is available from the British Library

Bible Story Time

Noah and the Flood

Sophie Piper ✱ Estelle Corke

LION
CHILDREN'S

Long ago, there lived a man named Noah. He and his wife had three sons. The three sons each had a wife.

"Perhaps I'll have grandchildren soon," said Noah to himself.

He began to dream of happy times ahead.

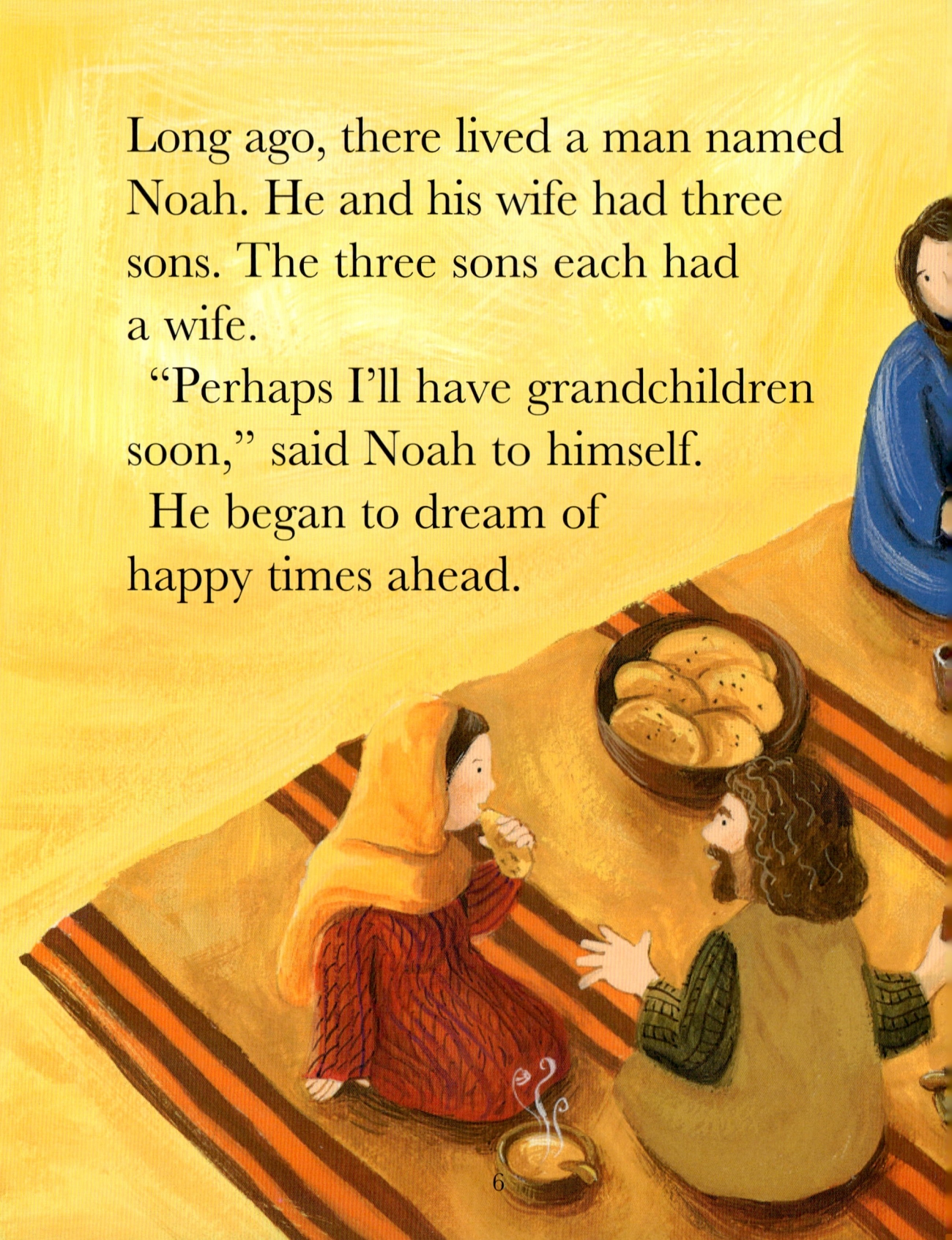

As Noah sat dreaming, he heard a voice.

"I am unhappy," said the voice. "I made a good world, but people nowadays do very bad things."

"Who's that speaking?" said Noah to himself. "The one who made the world, hmm?

"Oh! It must be God!"

"I want to begin the world again," said God to Noah. "I want you to help me."

Noah listened carefully to everything God said.

Then Noah went to talk to the family. "God wants us to build a boat," he said. "A very big boat. God has given me instructions and lots of measurements.

"Now to begin, we must fetch some good strong wood…"

The work began. Together they built a boat with three decks and a door. They put waterproof tar on the outside.

"Now we must fetch the animals," said Noah. "A mother and a father of every kind."

What a job it was! What a noisy job!

"We need food too," said Noah. "Food for us and food for the animals."

In the end, the work was done. Everyone and everything were safely on board.

God shut the door.

The rain started to fall. Pitter-patter, pitter-patter. Splish-splash.

Soon the rain was tumbling down. Splosh-splosh-splosh-splosh-splosh-splosh-splosh.

It rained and rained and rained. And rained.

The flood began to rise. Up and up and up. And up.

"Look," said Noah's wife, "the whole world is like one big sea."

"And there's only us left," said Noah.

He looked down at the grey water.

He looked up at the grey sky.

"I hope God hasn't forgotten us," said Noah.

God had not forgotten. God sent a wind that blew and blew.

Whoo-ooh, whoo-ooh, whoo-ooh.

Trickle by trickle, the flood began to go down until one day…

BUMP.

"We've landed," announced Noah. "Somewhere."

Not long after, they saw they were on a mountaintop. Noah sent a raven out from the boat. It flapped and flapped and flew away.

"I'll try again," said Noah. He sent a dove out from the boat. The first time it went, it flew out and flew back. The second time it went, the dove came back with an olive leaf.

Everyone on the ark cheered.

"The flood is over," said God. "Let the animals go. Tell them all to have families. I want them to fill the world again."

Out they went. What a noise!

"Now it's time for you to go," said God to Noah. "You and your family must make new homes for yourselves. You must fill the world with people again."

Out in the bright, clean world, Noah and his family had a big party.

"Look," said God. "I have put a rainbow in the sky. It is the sign of my promise. I will never flood the world again."

Noah smiled. Now he knew that for ever and ever there would be summer and winter.

For ever and ever there would be a time to sow seeds and a time to harvest crops.

God's world would be a home for his grandchildren, and his great grandchildren… for everyone.

Moses and the Princess

This

Bible Story Time book

belongs to

_____

_____

_____

Text by Sophie Piper
Illustrations copyright © 2005 Estelle Corke
This edition copyright © 2014 Lion Hudson

The right of Estelle Corke to be identified as the illustrator of this work has been asserted by her in accordance with the Copyright, Designs and Patents Act 1988.

All rights reserved. No part of this publication may be reproduced or transmitted in any form or by any means, electronic or mechanical, including photocopy, recording, or any information storage and retrieval system, without permission in writing from the publisher.

Published by Lion Children's Books
an imprint of
Lion Hudson plc
Wilkinson House, Jordan Hill Road,
Oxford OX2 8DR, England
www.lionhudson.com/lionchildrens

ISBN 978 0 7459 6946 6

First edition 2005
This edition 2014

This book is part of a box set and is not to be sold separately

A catalogue record for this book is available from the British Library

Bible Story Time

Moses and the Princess

Sophie Piper * Estelle Corke

LION CHILDREN'S

Miriam smiled at her new baby brother.

"He's very special, isn't he?" she said to her mother.

"Very special," said her mother. "We must both take very good care of him."

There was a problem. Miriam and her family were Israelites. Long ago, the Israelites had been invited to live in Egypt. Now there were lots of them and the Egyptians were afraid of them.

They made them work as slaves.

The king had made a law that all Israelite baby boys must be thrown into the river. His soldiers often came looking.

Miriam's mother made a basket from reeds. She covered it with waterproof tar. She put the baby in the basket and went down to the river.

She hid her baby in his little basket among the reeds.

Miriam hid close by to watch what would happen.

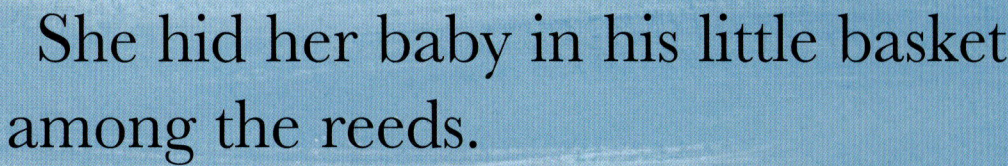

The daughter of the king of Egypt came down to the river to bathe. Her servants stood on the bank.

Suddenly, the princess saw the basket.

"Please fetch that for me," she said. "I want to know what's inside."

When the princess lifted the lid, she saw the baby boy.

"Poor little thing! He's crying!" she said. "He's an Israelite baby. Someone wants to keep him safe. I'd like to keep him."

Miriam stepped forward. She spoke up bravely: "If you like, I can find an Israelite woman to take care of him for you."

"Yes please," replied the princess.

Miriam ran home and called to her mother.

"Come quickly," she said. "The princess found our baby. She wants to keep him. She needs someone to look after him."

The two hurried back as fast as they could. The princess gave the mother her own baby.

"Please look after him for me," she said. "I will pay you. When the boy is old enough, he will come and live at the palace."

"His name –" began the mother.

"Oh, yes: what shall I call him?" said the princess. "I know: Moses."

Moses grew up to be a prince. He lived among the Egyptians.

He was rich and powerful.

But he knew he was really an Israelite.

He was very angry at the way his people were treated. That got him into trouble, and he had to run away.

In the faraway desert, Moses became a shepherd. One day he saw a strange sight: a bush was on fire, but none of it was really burning.

The fire was a sign that God was there. God spoke to Moses.

"I want you to rescue my people. Tell the king of Egypt to let them go free."

Moses went and asked his brother Aaron to help him. Together they went to see the king of Egypt.

"If you don't let our people go, God will send all sorts of trouble," they pleaded.

"No," said the king. "No, no, no and no."

There was one disaster after another: frogs hopping everywhere, flies buzzing everywhere, locusts chewing everywhere. The king would not change his mind.

The troubles got worse. The king changed his mind. Moses led his people out of Egypt, away from the cruel king.

Suddenly, the king changed his mind again. "Hurry!" he told his army. "Drive your chariots as fast as you can. Go and get them back."

The people saw the army behind them.

They saw a sea in front of them. Moses lifted his stick, and God made a path for them through the sea.

Safe on the other side, Miriam danced and played the tambourine. "God has saved us," she sang, and everyone joined in.

David and Goliath

This
Bible Story Time book
belongs to

_____

_____

_____

Text by Sophie Piper
Illustrations copyright © 2005 Estelle Corke
This edition copyright © 2014 Lion Hudson

The right of Estelle Corke to be identified as the illustrator of this work has been asserted by her in accordance with the Copyright, Designs and Patents Act 1988.

All rights reserved. No part of this publication may be reproduced or transmitted in any form or by any means, electronic or mechanical, including photocopy, recording, or any information storage and retrieval system, without permission in writing from the publisher.

Published by Lion Children's Books
an imprint of
Lion Hudson plc
Wilkinson House, Jordan Hill Road,
Oxford OX2 8DR, England
www.lionhudson.com/lionchildrens

ISBN 978 0 7459 6946 6

First edition 2005
This edition 2014

This book is part of a box set and is not to be sold separately

A catalogue record for this book is available from the British Library

Bible Story Time

David and Goliath

Sophie Piper ✱ Estelle Corke

LION
CHILDREN'S

David was the youngest in his family. Like everyone, he had to help on the family farm.

His job was to look after the sheep. While he watched them, he liked to sing. Sometimes he played his harp.

Sometimes he practiced throwing stones with his sling.

He was a good shot.

He needed to be a good shot: sometimes wild animals came and tried to steal his sheep.

David slung stones at them to make them go away.

One day, David's father sent him on an errand.

"Your brothers have been away in the king's army for a long time. Go to see if they are well. They will not have much food left. Here is bread and cheese to take them."

David set off. He found the soldiers lining up, ready to fight.

David hurried to find his brothers.

Across the valley, an enemy soldier was marching forward. He wore heavy armor. He carried a huge spear.

"I am Goliath!" shouted the enemy soldier. "Come and fight me! Beat me, and you will win the war. Lose, and you will become our slaves.

"Ha, ha, ha! Ha, ha, ha! Ha, ha, ha!"

The king's soldiers began to run. "Look at him!" they said to each other.

"Would you fight that giant soldier? The king will give a big reward to the man who does."

"Tell me more!" said David eagerly. "We shouldn't be scared. We are God's people."

One of David's brothers heard him talking. "Little brat!" he said. "You should be at home with the sheep."

David kept asking questions.
Someone took him to see King Saul.

"Your Majesty," said David. "No one should be afraid of that soldier. I will go and fight him."

Saul sighed. "You're just a boy!" he said.

"I can fight bears and lions," said David. "I stop them stealing my sheep."

In the end, the king let David go. He took his stick and his sling.

He stopped by a stream to pick up five small pebbles.

Goliath came marching down. His shield bearer marched in front of him.

"Come on! Come and fight!" jeered Goliath. "You'll be a tasty meal for the vultures!"

David stood up. "You've got a sword, a spear, and a javelin," he called. "But I trust in God."

Then he put a stone in his sling.

He whirled the sling above his head.

He threw the stone.

It hit Goliath sharply. The giant fell down.

The army behind David cheered. "We've won! We've won!"

The enemy army in front of David began to run away. Saul's army chased them all the way back to their own cities.

David became a famous soldier. He won many battles for his people.

When King Saul died, David became the next king.

He had a beautiful palace. He was very rich.

He didn't have to worry about sheep. He didn't have to worry about wild animals.

He still liked singing. He still liked playing the harp.

He still put his trust in God.

"I shall write a song," he said to himself. "It will tell everyone about God and God's goodness."

*Dear God, you are my shepherd,
You give me all I need,
You take me where the grass
 grows green
And I can safely feed.*

*You take me where the water
Is quiet and cool and clear;
And there I rest and know I'm safe
For you are always near.*

Jonah and the Whale

This
Bible Story Time book
belongs to

_____

_____

_____

Text by Sophie Piper
Illustrations copyright © 2005 Estelle Corke
This edition copyright © 2014 Lion Hudson

The right of Estelle Corke to be identified as the illustrator of this work has been asserted by her in accordance with the Copyright, Designs and Patents Act 1988.

All rights reserved. No part of this publication may be reproduced or transmitted in any form or by any means, electronic or mechanical, including photocopy, recording, or any information storage and retrieval system, without permission in writing from the publisher.

Published by Lion Children's Books
an imprint of
Lion Hudson plc
Wilkinson House, Jordan Hill Road,
Oxford OX2 8DR, England
www.lionhudson.com/lionchildrens

ISBN 978 0 7459 6946 6

First edition 2005
This edition 2014

This book is part of a box set and is not to be sold separately

A catalogue record for this book is available from the British Library

Bible Story Time

Jonah and the Whale

Sophie Piper ✳ Estelle Corke

LION
CHILDREN'S

Jonah was a prophet. When God spoke, Jonah listened. Then he told other people God's message.

One particular day, God asked Jonah to do something.

"Go to Nineveh. The people there do wicked things. Tell them I've noticed how bad they are."

Jonah frowned. "Hmph," he said. "The people of Nineveh are our enemies."

"In fact," he said to himself, "I won't go."

Jonah knew which road led to Nineveh. He went the other way, to a town called Joppa.

Down by the harbor was a boat. It was ready to sail to Spain.

"I'll go there!" said Jonah.

He paid his fare and climbed on board.

That night, a storm blew up.

"RRAAHH," roared the wind.

"CRRRASSHH," went the waves.

"Help! We're sinking," cried the sailors. "Help! Help!"

The captain found Jonah asleep.

"Get up and pray!" he ordered. "Ask your god to save us."

The sailors were all praying, but the storm grew worse.

"A powerful god is angry with one of us," said a sailor. "Let's do the choosing game to find out who."

It was Jonah.

"I'm sorry," he said. "I'm running away from God. You'll have to throw me overboard."

The sailors tried to row the ship to shore, but it was no good.

They shouted to heaven. "O God, whoever you are, we're really sorry. Please don't blame us!"

Then they picked Jonah up and threw him into the sea.

Splash!

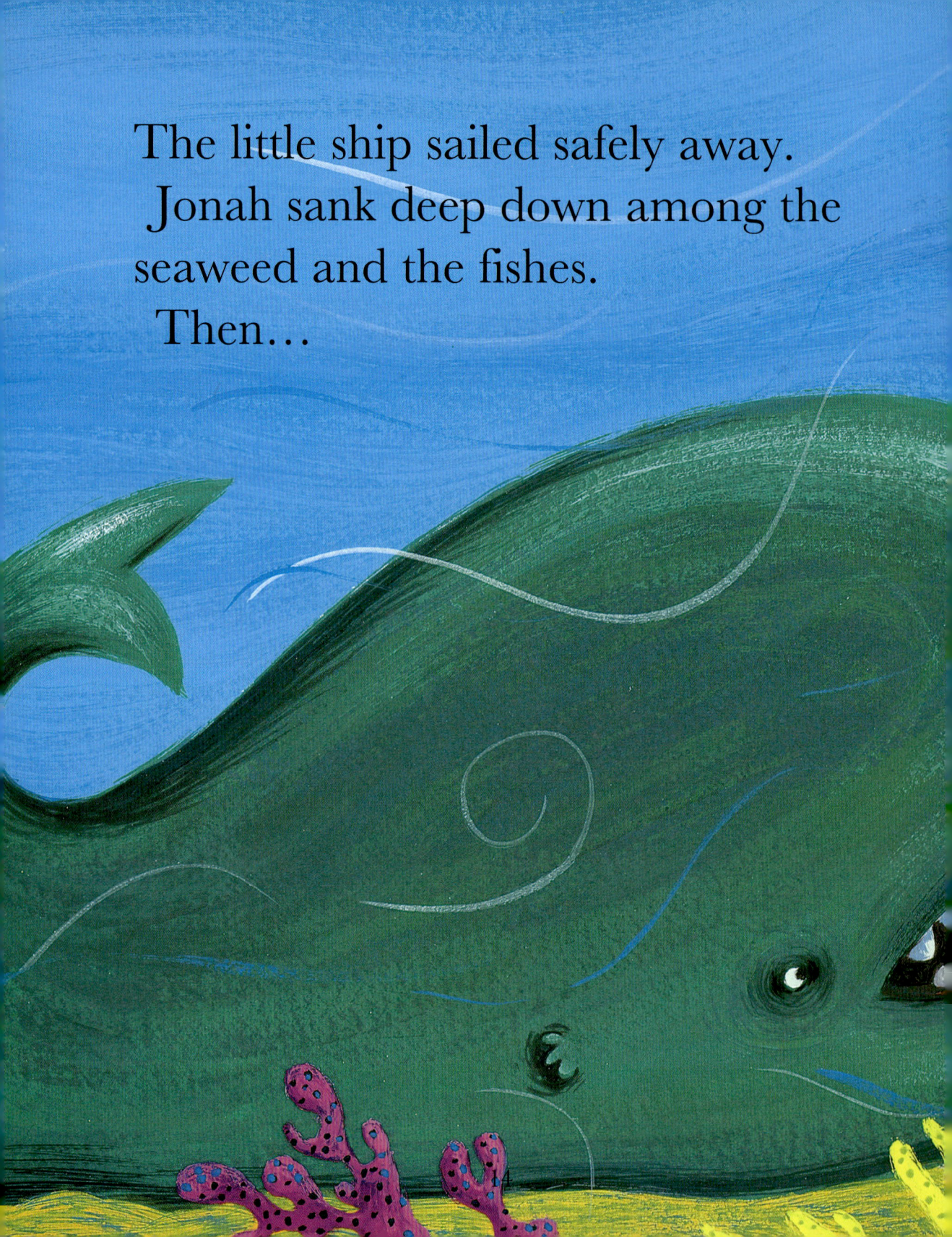

The little ship sailed safely away. Jonah sank deep down among the seaweed and the fishes.
Then…

"Oh," said Jonah. "I thought that was the end of me. But suddenly everything has changed.

"I think I've been swallowed by an enormous fish.

"It must be a miracle. Well… in that case, I'd better say a prayer."

He began.

"Thank you, God, for saving me. I'm very sorry. Please keep me alive, and then I'll do what you want."

He waited and waited and waited. Then he felt himself being thrown forward.

"Help!" he began.

The fish spat Jonah onto a beach.

Splot

Jonah went straight to Nineveh.
"Listen up, you Ninevites!" cried Jonah. "God says this: you have been very wicked. In forty days, God will destroy your city."

"Oh my!" said the people of Nineveh. "Oh dear! Oh no! Oh help!"

The king of Nineveh called all the people together.

"Listen everyone," he announced. "We must show God we are sorry.

"No one is to eat anything. Everyone is to wear scratchy sackcloth. All of us must pray to God.

"Most of all, we must stop doing wicked things. Then, perhaps, God will forgive us."

"I'm pleased," said God. "I think I'll forgive them."

Jonah heard what God said and it made him angry.

"I knew it, God," he said. "That's what I was afraid you'd do."

Jonah stomped out of the city.

He found a place to sit. He wanted to watch what happened next.

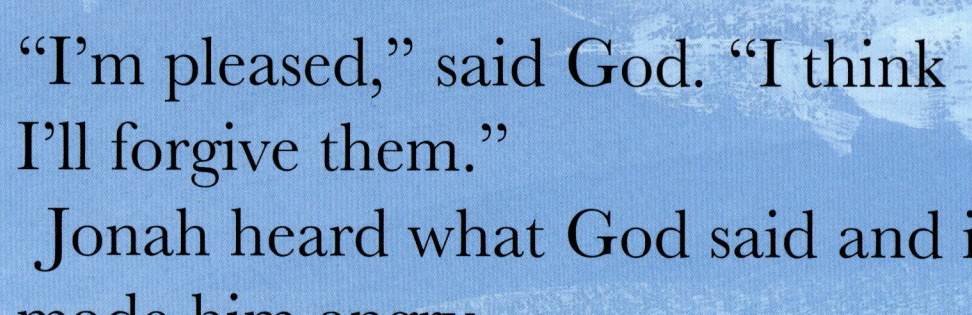

The sun shone brightly.

"Phew, it's hot here," he said to himself. "I need to make a shelter."

He worked all day. The shelter was good, but Jonah was still hot.

"I wish there was some shade," he said. "Oh… look at that plant! It's growing before my very eyes."

Jonah watched as the plant grew around his shelter. He watched the leaves unfold. They were huge and gave lovely cool shade.

"This is very nice," said Jonah. "Perhaps things aren't so bad after all."

The next day, Jonah heard a sound.

Munch,
munch,
munch!

A worm came and chewed the stem and the leaves. Very soon, the plant died.

"My poor plant!" cried Jonah. "Now I'll have no shade when the sun gets hot."

The day grew hotter and hotter.
"It's horrible out here," said Jonah.
"I wish I were dead."

Then he heard God speaking.

"Why are you angry about the plant, Jonah?

"I was the one who made it grow for you. You did nothing. Yet you feel sorry for it."

"I do indeed!" said Jonah.

"I made the people of Nineveh," said God. "There are thousands of them. Grown ups, children – and all their animals. I feel sorry for them. That is why I am going to forgive them."

Daniel and the Lions

This
Bible Story Time book
belongs to

_____

_____

_____

Text by Sophie Piper
Illustrations copyright © 2005 Estelle Corke
This edition copyright © 2014 Lion Hudson

The right of Estelle Corke to be identified as the illustrator of this work has been asserted by her in accordance with the Copyright, Designs and Patents Act 1988.

All rights reserved. No part of this publication may be reproduced or transmitted in any form or by any means, electronic or mechanical, including photocopy, recording, or any information storage and retrieval system, without permission in writing from the publisher.

Published by Lion Children's Books
an imprint of
Lion Hudson plc
Wilkinson House, Jordan Hill Road,
Oxford OX2 8DR, England
www.lionhudson.com/lionchildrens

ISBN 978 0 7459 6946 6

First edition 2005
This edition 2014

This book is part of a box set and is not to be sold separately

A catalogue record for this book is available from the British Library

Bible Story Time

Daniel and the Lions

Sophie Piper ✶ Estelle Corke

LION
CHILDREN'S

Daniel was a very important man. He helped King Darius rule his empire.

He worked hard, and he was very good at his job.

"I think I shall put Daniel in charge of the empire," said Darius.

The other people who worked for Darius were very angry.

"Why is Daniel getting a better job?" they muttered. "How we wish he would make a big mistake! Then we could get rid of him."

"You know," said one, "I've got an idea. Listen to my secret plan."
They huddled close together and whispered.

Then they went to King Darius.

"Your Majesty," they said. "May you live for ever.

"You are great. You are wonderful. You are like a god."

"Thank you very much," said Darius.

"We want you to make a law," said the men. "No one may pray to anyone except to you. If anyone disobeys, they will be thrown into a den of lions."

"What a wonderful idea," said Darius. "It will be one of my great laws that cannot be changed."

Daniel always prayed to God.

In the morning, he prayed to God.

In the middle of the day, he prayed to God.

At the end of the day, he said this prayer:

*"When I lie down, I sleep in peace.
Dear God, you always keep me safe."*

Daniel was not alone. The people he worked with were watching.

The next day, they went to see King Darius.

"Your Majesty," they said. "May you live for ever.

"Do you remember the law you made?"

"I do," said Darius. "It's a very strict law: no ifs, no buts, no changes."

"Indeed it is," said the men. "If anyone breaks it, you will throw them into a den of lions."

"I will," said Darius. Then, for a bit of fun, he roared. "Hooraaaaaah!"

"Your Majesty," said the men. "Daniel has broken the law. He keeps on saying prayers to his God."

Darius stopped making roaring noises. He looked very sad. "I don't want Daniel eaten," he said. "He's a very good worker. He's not included in the law."

"Oh, but Your Majesty," said the men. "You CANNOT change the law."

Darius frowned. "Let me think," he said. "I'm going to find a reason why he shouldn't be included."

He was thinking as the sun rose high in the sky. One of the men popped in to see him.

"Daniel's saying his midday prayers," said the man.

"Go away, I'm still thinking," said Darius.

He was thinking as the sun sank low. The same man popped back.

"Daniel's saying his evening prayers," he said.

"Oh dear," said Darius. "It's the den for Daniel."

Soldiers went to fetch Daniel and threw him to the lions.

Darius came to see him. "It's all a bit of a mistake," he called to Daniel. "I hope your God will keep you safe."

"Excuse me, Your Majesty," said a soldier. "Please move along. I'm going to block the opening to the den.

"We don't want anyone to let Daniel out, do we?"

Darius did not sleep that night.
"Oh dear, oh dear, oh dear," he muttered. He paced up and down.
"Do you want a meal?" asked a servant. "Or some wine?"

"No thank you," said the king.

"Shall I play some music for you?" asked another servant.

"Stop trying to cheer me up," said Darius. "It just makes me more angry."

Down in the pit, Daniel was sitting among the shadows. He couldn't see anything very clearly, but he felt sure someone was there with him. Whoever it was seemed to have a special power over the lions.

First they yawned huge, scary yawns. Then they gave little growls and fell asleep.

As soon as it was light, the king hurried to the pit.

"Daniel?" he called. "Did your God save you?"

"May Your Majesty live for ever!" replied Daniel. "God sent an angel to save me from the lions."

"Hoorah!" cried Darius. This time, he didn't roar.

He helped pull Daniel to safety. "Fetch the men who tried to kill Daniel," he said to the soldiers. "Put them in the pit instead."

Then King Darius sent a message to everyone in his empire.

"There is no god like Daniel's God.

"Daniel's God is strong and works miracles to save people.

"Everyone must respect Daniel's God."

Daniel went back to his old job, and he did it very, very well.